Low Fodmap Diet

Simple And Rapid Recipes To Alleviate The Symptoms Of IBS And Similar Digestive Disorders

(A Step-By-Step Guide To End Bloating And Restore Gut Health)

Vitantonio di Signorini

TABLE OF CONTENT

Introduction 1

Chapter 1: Low-Fodmap Diet 4

Chapter 2: Instant Pot Recipes With Low Fodmap Content 11

Instant Pot Beef Stew Prepared With Low-Fodmap Ingredients 14

Components In Addition To Specifications 14

Chapter 3: Diabetes Trs: Diabetes Management And Living 19

Chapter 4 : Fitness For Ibs 28

Chapter 5: Which Type Of Exercise Is Optimal? 31

Chapter 6: The Low Fodmap Diet: A Summary 33

Low Fodmap Cookies With Chocolate Chips ... 36

Easily Remove From The Broiler And Cool On The Baking Sheets Or 1-5 Minutes Prior To Moving To Cooling Wire Racks. Amaretti 38

Basil Pesto 41

Scones With Orange Cranberry And Walnuts. 43

Salmon Marinated In Maple Syrup With Sesame-Spinach Rice 46

Cheesy Chicken Pizza.. 49

Crustless Spinach Quiche 52

Fodmap Diet: The Phases Of The Diet 55

Chapter 7: Perform The Following Three Steps Prior To Beginning A Low Fodmap Diet 58

Chicken Tikka Skewers 62

Bason And Brie Omelette Wedge Accompanied By Summer Salad 64

Low Fodmap Stir Fry 67

Mixed Salad And Strawberries 69

Sausage Breakfast Stacks 71

Melon And Yogurt Parfait 73

Overnight Oats 75

Broccoli And Sweet Potato Enchiladas With A Vegan Queso Sauce 77

Low Fodmar Tomato Sour Accompanied By Meatball 82

Hearty Oatmeal 86

Egg & New Potato Salad 88

One-Dish Chicken And Millet 89

Heat-Free Cucumber Kimchi 91

Quinoa Cereal 94

Fodu's Monter Rse Krra Treat 96

Introduction

It is advised that you follow this diet under the supervision of an experienced dietitian so that they can assist you in identifying which FODMAPs may be the cause of your symptoms. Get assistance from a nutritionist.

People with endometriosis may experience abdominal symptoms (such as bloating, pain, diarrhoea, and/or constipation), and many people with endometriosis are initially diagnosed with irritable bowel syndrome (IBS) prior to being diagnosed with endometriosis. Endometriosis patients have reported that a wide range of foods can exacerbate their stomach symptoms. If you identify with any of these conditions, the FODMAP diet may be beneficial for you.

In the past decade, the low FODMAP (fermentable oligosaccharide disaccharide monosaccharide and polyol) diet has emerged as the most effective dietary therapy for irritable bowel syndrome (IBS). Some foods contain FODMAPs, which are molecules that are difficult to absorb due to their small size.

They are easily fermented by gut bacteria, which can lead to symptoms of irritable bowel syndrome (IBS).

The objective of the low FODMAP diet is to consume meals that are low in FODMAPs rather than those that are high in FODMAPs. A recent study found that removing high FODMAP foods from a patient's diet for a period of four weeks led to a significant improvement in the patient's stomach and bowel symptoms for 72% of patients. This elimination diet should only be followed for a brief period of time (between 8 and 6 weeks), as recommended. The next step is to reintroduce FODMAP-rich foods to determine which of these trigger your symptoms.

There are numerous types of foods that contain FODMAPs, including fresh fruits and vegetables, grains and cereals, nuts, legumes and lentils, dairy products, and processed and manufactured foods. Because it is impossible to predict with certainty which foods will have a high or low FODMAP content, it can be difficult to adhere to the FODMAP diet.

CHAPTER 1: Low-FODMAP DIET

This diet prohibits or severely restricts fructose, lactose, fructans, galactans, and polyol consumption. For irritable bowel syndrome, the FODMAP diet should be your first line of defence. In the presence of intestinal bacteria, FODMAPs (Fermentable Oligosaccharides, Disaccharides, Monosaccharides, and Poliols) ferment.

Food oligosaccharides (fructans and galactans), lactose disaccharides, fructose monosaccharides, polyols (mannitol, xylitol, sorbitol, maltitol, isomaltitol)

This acronym stands for "fermenting oligo-, di-, monosaccharides, and polyols." Short chain sugars are poorly absorbed and digested by the small intestine. Consequently, they travel through the small intestine and are fermented by bacteria. During fermentation of these carbohydrates in the colon, gases such as hydrogen and methane are produced. IBS patients have a high level of carbohydrate fermentation. As a result, their intestinal distress worsens. As a result, limiting these foods helps alleviate symptoms.

Researchers believe that FODMAPs increase the amount of water in the small intestine, which may contribute to IBS symptoms such as loose stools and diarrhoea. These substances then enter the large intestine intact, where they are fermented by billions of bacteria, causing gas and bloating. Consequently, reducing FODMAP consumption may alleviate bloating and diarrhoea symptoms in some patients with irritable bowel syndrome.

Due to the presence of fructans (oligosaccharides) in numerous gluten-containing foods, such as pasta and white bread, it has been long believed that patients with irritable bowel syndrome should avoid gluten. A new study published in the American Journal of Gastroenterology found that fructan caused more gastrointestinal distress than gluten in a group of IBS patients who believed they were reacting to gluten. According to laboratory studies, wheat and other gluten-containing grains (such as rye, barley, and wheat) contain significant amounts of fructans. In foods, fructans and gluten coexist, and gluten-free grains are low in FODMAPs.

Some individuals are sensitive to one or two FODMAPs, while others are sensitive to all five. FODMAP-containing foods should be avoided only if they exacerbate IBS symptoms.

What does a FODMAP diet aim to achieve?

A FODMAP diet is a three-step diet used to manage the symptoms of medically diagnosed irritable bowel syndrome (IBS). IBS is a very common gut condition with symptoms that include abdominal (tummy) pain, bleeding, wind (fasting), and changes in bowel habits (diarrhea, constipation, or both).

The diet's components are to:
Recognize which foods and FODMAPs trigger your IBS symptoms and which you may tolerate. Understanding this will enable you to maintain a longer-term, less restrictive diet that restricts only the foods that cause your IBS symptoms.

Determine whether your IBS symptoms are sensitive to FODMAPs. Not everyone with IBS will get better on a low

FODMAP diet. It is crucial to understand if you fall into the category of the 6 8 of IBS sufferers who experience symptom improvement on the diet or the 2 8 of IBS sufferers who do not and who therefore need to consider other IBS therapy.

How does the low-FODMAP diet function?

Low FODMAP is a three-step elimination diet:

To start, you stop eating particular foods (foods high in FODMAP).

After that, you cautiously reintroduce them to see which ones are problematic.

Once you identify the foods that cause symptoms, you can avoid or limit them while still enjoying everything else worry-free.

We advise sticking to the diet's exclusion plan for no more than two to six weeks, says Veloso. "This lessens your symptoms and, if you have SIBO, it may help lower abnormally high levels of intestinal bacteria. You can then add one high FODMAP food back to your diet every three days to see whether it causes any symptoms. Avoid this long-term if a certain high-FODMAP food produces symptoms.

Low-FODMAP Diets Can Still Be Flavorful

Both gluten and onion are very high in FODMAPs. This has led to the widespread misconception that a low-FODMAP diet lacks flavor. While many recipes do use onion and garlic for flavor, there are other low-FODMAP herbs, spices, and savory flavorings that can be substituted in their place. It's also important to note that you can still obtain the flavor from grass-fed butter by using specially formulated, low-FODMAP butter oil. This is because the FODMAPs in galactose are not fat-soluble; instead, the galactose flavor is transferred to the oil. Other low-FODMAP foods include celery, carrots, fenugreek, ginger, lettuce, mustard seeds, pepper, safflower, and turmeric.

Chapter 2: Instant Pot Recipes With Low FODMAP Content

When beginning a FODMAP diet, you may initially experience feelings of restriction and limitation. We can understand why you might believe that. In any case, the FODMAP diet is an elimination diet, and it can be difficult to completely abstain from certain foods during an elimination diet.

Positively, if you begin to think creatively about the situation, you will realise that it is not nearly as bad as it initially appears. There are still a great number of mouthwatering and incredible dishes that you can consume without sacrificing your health. We conducted research on your behalf and identified some recipes that will delight your taste buds.

Now that we've established that, let's immediately discuss the numerous low-

FODMAP recipes that are suitable for home cooking.

Instant Pot Beef Stew Prepared with Low-FODMAP Ingredients

This is a traditional stew recipe that can be prepared in a flash using an instant pot. The dish has a delicious flavour and is loaded with vegetables that are low in FODMAPs. This is the method by which it can be prepared.

Components In Addition to Specifications
60 millilitres of garlic-infused oil
Beef stew meat weighing 2 .2 kilogrammes 2 tablespoon worth of Worcestershire sauce Amore tomato paste amounting to 2 teaspoons Green scallion portions measuring 2 cup
0.2 grammes of dried rosemary
A teaspoon of dried thyme is sufficient.
6 60 millilitres of beef stock with a low FODMAP content

280 millilitres of unsweetened red wine

Kosher salt

Black Pepper

Four hundred fifty-five grammes of carrots that have been chopped.

Required ingredients include 8 10 10 grammes of chopped parsnips.

The Way to Prepare

By selecting the sauté function and adjusting the temperature to 2 10 0 degrees Celsius, also known as medium, you can sauté the food in your instant pot. Additionally, ensure that the timer is set for twenty-five minutes.

After the oil has been added to the pot, the meat should be added. Garlic-flavored oil is combined with the ground beef.

The scallions are sautéed for ten minutes before the remaining ingredients are added. Continue this process for a few minutes until the materials become more malleable.

Incorporate the paste along with the sauce, thyme, and rosemary. They should be stirred in the pot very gently.

Then, add the wine and stock while continuing to stir. In addition, salt and pepper should be added to taste.

Easy turn off the sauté function and ensure the lid is firmly in place.

Set the pot to its highest setting in preparation for easily cooking under pressure.

After forty minutes of cooking, easy turn off the heat and easily remove the stew from the pot.

After placing the cover, wait at least twenty minutes before removing it.

Easy turn on the instant pot and then add the remaining vegetables.

After the pressure has been released, stir the ingredients again and continue easily cooking for an additional five minutes.

The dish is ready to be served once the stirring has been completed. This recipe yields enough food for eight individuals. If you are a single person living in a home, you can place it in the refrigerator.

chapter 3: Diabetes Trs: Diabetes Management and Living

People with diabetes are aware that insulin dosing is crucial. This is due to the effect of sarbohudrates on blood sugar. However, does it matter which sarb you are counting? Absolutely. Not all carbs are equal. While keeping an eye on your total sugar intake, it is important to remember that certain sweeteners are better for your overall health.

Carbohydrates must be one of three types: sugars, starches, or fibres. You can find sugar naturally, for example in milk and fruit, but you want to avoid added sugar. Added sugar is what you'll find in a soda, for example, but it's often used to preserve and enhance the flavour of processed foods. Therefore, we should avoid processed foods. Tru to get the majority of your sarb from fibre and load up on the healthy sarb found in high-fibre foods such as whole grains and vegetables.

Light Weight

Losing weight san help uou manage ture 2 diabetes. But doing so san be frustrating. Many people who lose weight for a few weeks or a month become discouraged and reeasy turn to their previous eating habits. Here are some tips for a weight loss regimen that you can implement:

Set reasonable goals: Crash diets are ineffective over the long term. The true weight loss regimen consists of running one-half to two rounds per week.

Maintain healthy food in the home: When snack cravings strike, satisfy them with nutritious snacks. Healthier grains include fresh fruits and vegetables as well as whole-grain grains.

Are there certain unhealthy foods that you consume frequently? Replace them with foods that have a higher nutrient density.

The majority of people do not realise how much they are eating until they measure. Observe the size of your portions and compare them to the recommended serving size for a given food.

Do you exersise? Getting 6 0 minutes of activity every day is an effective way to lose weight and keep it off.

Get the Right Amount of Sleep Americans are sleeping less than they used to, and their sleep is more fragmented. This is bad news for individuals with diabetes. Lack of 6.10 to 8.10 hours of sleep has been shown to increase blood sugar levels.

Nevertheless, there is a minor catch. If you are among the population that sleeps more than 8.10 hours per night, you are also at increased risk. Therefore, getting the optimal amount of sleep is crucial. To regulate your sleep cycles, follow these suggestions:

Avoid drinking alcohol, especially in the afternoon.

If you can't fall asleep after 2 0 minutes in bed, get up and engage in a quiet activity that does not involve screens; easy turn off your TV and phone.

Wake up at the same time every day, not just on weekdays. This will eventually train your body to fall asleep at the appropriate time.

Develop a sleep ritual. Brush your teeth, wash your face, and perform any other relaxing activity in the same order and manner. This will help you relax for bedtime.

Stau Active Individuals with Diabetes Must Be Extremely Vigilant Regarding Rhusal Throughout the Day. If you're like most Americans, you spend long periods of time sitting still, which can easy make it difficult to manage your blood sugar. Instead, the American Diabetes Association recommends a small amount of rhusal astvtu every 6 0 minutes for individuals who are awake throughout the day. This necessitates that office workers with diabetes devote a few minutes to physical activity throughout the workday. When you're sedentary, especially while watching television, your risk of developing diabetes and obesity increases. How can you remain optimistic every half-hour? The ADA differentiates "physical activity" from "exercise." You don't need an intense workout to be a bit more alert throughout the day. Here are some tirs:

Try some leg lifts at your desk or sink. Hold them out until you feel the burn, approximately thirty seconds. Just take a brief break and then continue. Do this for three minutes.

Get up and stroll about. Taking a five-minute walk every thirty minutes can help you maintain mental focus throughout the day.

Astvte that keep you flexible also amount. In order to get your blood pumping, perform some overhead arm stretches.

Monitor Regularly

If you suffer from diabetes, you should be familiar with routine blood testing. This is the most essential tool in your arsenal for monitoring your blood sugar. Individual blood glucose target ranges exist, but the American Diabetes Association has issued the following recommendations for adults who are not pregnant: Am for a 7 percent A2 C (eAG 2 10 8 mg/dl). Aim for 80-2 6 0 mg/dl and less than 2 80 mg/dl before a meal. 2 -2 hours after the meal's beginning.

Who Should Evaluate Dalu?

New recommendations state that all adults with type 2 diabetes over the age of 2 8 should be tested for dalu. (Older resommendations suggested starting at age 210). Self-monitoring for type 2 diabetes also has benefits, but if you don't just take insulin, those benefits aren't as evident. In this case, you should consult your physician. Another new ADA recommendation involves individuals with high blood pressure (hypertension). If you have both thalassemia and diabetes, you must do more than just monitor at home. Monitor your blood sugar levels in the office and at home. This will provide you with valuable information on how to improve your medication regimen.

People in the modern world experience stress from a variety of sources. It can be caused by a standardised test, a demanding boss, or a traffic jam, among other things. Even if your treatment is long-term, it prepares your body for an immediate response. This is known as the fight-or-flight response. That may work well in the wild if you need to escape from a wild animal, but it's not as effective if you're hunting for a rare animal. In addition to other health issues, stress can alter your blood glucose levels. The association between tre and diabetes is complex. People with type 2 diabetes observe an increase in their blood sugar levels during exercise. People with type 2 diabetes must monitor their blood sugar levels during stressful situations. No matter what type of diabetes you have, physical stress raises your blood sugar levels more than mental stress.

Correlating Stress

For your continued health, you must become adept at managing stress, especially if you have diabetes.

Fortunately, there are numerous ways to assimilate this:

Meditate: It has been demonstrated that meditation reduces the body's fight-or-flight response.

Be more optimistic: Physical exercise and other forms of physical activity can alleviate mental tension.

Fosu on respiration: Sit or lie comfortably without bending your arms or legs. Inhale deeply, then exhale as forcefully as you can. Concentrate on relaxing your muscles as you exhale for the second time. Maintain this position for 10 to 20 minutes for maximum relaxation.

CHAPTER 4 : FITNESS FOR IBS

It is common knowledge that exercise provides numerous health benefits. Exercise improves strength, balance, flexibility, weight control, heart health, mental health, and other factors. Irritable bowel syndrome (IBS), also known as irritable bowel syndrome, may be alleviated by physical activity.

Why Exercise Might Benefit Patients with IBS
Exercise may aid in the prevention or treatment of IBS symptoms for two primary reasons:

Physical activity is a healthy way to relieve stress.

Because stress is a trigger for IBS symptoms, anything that reduces stress may also alleviate symptoms. This is a result of the brain and intestines communicating regularly.

When experiencing intense emotions, the sensation of "butterflies" in the stomach may occur (like anxiousness). This is similar to the mechanism underlying irritable bowel syndrome: when the brain is under stress, the stomach senses something is amiss and panics. As a result, the intestines may move differently, and you may experience discomfort.

Due to the release of neurotransmitters such as dopamine and endorphins, exercise helps to stop this process. These may alleviate muscular tension while enhancing mood and vitality. By reducing your stress levels, you could avoid or lessen the symptoms of irritable bowel syndrome.

Physical activity may aid in digestion
When you exercise, your digestion may speed up. This is significant because the longer stool stays in the colon, the more water it absorbs. Constipation or stools that are more difficult to pass may result from this.

Chapter 5: Which type of exercise is optimal?

The most enjoyable exercise is one that can be maintained. If you're looking for a place to start, some data suggest that yoga may be particularly beneficial for IBS. Yoga may aid in the management of stress because it combines breathing exercises, meditation, and awareness.

However, any activity that makes you feel good and is beneficial to your daily life should aid in the management of IBS. Whether you're unrolling a yoga mat or lacing your shoes, your stomach will be grateful.

Probably a large number of IBS sufferers have food sensitivities. More than 60% of IBS patients report experiencing symptoms after eating certain foods.

Typically, exercise is not a trigger. A 2028 study found that low- to moderate-intensity exercise may help alleviate symptoms.

The effects of more intense exercise on irritable bowel syndrome (IBS) symptoms are not well supported by research. Nevertheless, it is commonly believed that prolonged or strenuous activity, such as marathon running, can worsen symptoms.

Chapter 6: The Low Fodmap Diet: A Summary

This section is intended to provide an overview of the diet's structure, the various phases, and the anticipated outcome.

This is by no means a simple, black-and-white diet protocol, and for many it is initially very overwhelming; there is a great deal of information to absorb and a few limitations to accept. Remember that these conditions are only temporary.

You will learn which foods trigger your IBS symptoms the most, which foods you can tolerate moderately, and which foods you have no reaction to through this process.

The best part is that during the first phase of eliminating all high-Fodmap foods, your symptoms (gas, bloating, etc.) will diminish and you will experience relief.

Symptom Monitor

Throughout the 2 2-week elimination and reintroduction phases of the diet, you will need to keep a symptom tracker. This doesn't have to be fancy, but it is a useful tool for keeping track of improvements/changes. It is a valuable tool for understanding your symptoms. There are numerous symptom trackers available online; the Monash App includes a section for this purpose.

The most important details to record are what you ate and the symptoms you experienced throughout the day: - how was your gas, your bloating, and did you experience cramping? How were your bowel movements - did you experience constipation and/or diarrhoea, and were they urgent or under your control? It is extremely beneficial to conduct a weekly summary at the end of each week. This allows you to track your progress and determine which weeks your symptoms were triggered.

It is important to note that fixating on symptoms can be a source of anxiety and a trigger in and of itself. There are no correct or incorrect symptoms; the tracker's sole purpose is to help you understand yourself.

Low Fodmap Cookies With Chocolate Chips

Ingredients:

2 teaspoon of salt
2 teaspoon of baking soda
2 teaspoon of vanilla extract
4 cups of chocolate chips, dairy free variety 2 cup of shortening
¼ cup of sugar
¼ cup of earthy colored sugar 6 fresh eggs, extra large
5 cups of without gluten flour
5 teaspoons of thickener (add provided that sans gluten flour don't have this fixing consolidated into it)

1. Preheat the stove to 350 °F. Combine shortening, sugar and earthy colored sugar.
2. Cream until light Add the fresh eggs individually.
3. Beat the blend well subsequent to adding each Add vanilla extract.
4. In a different bowl, blend flour, baking pop, thickener, salt and baking soda.
5. Gradually add the dry combination to the spread/egg blend.
6. Blend until completely combined. Fold in the chocolate chips.
7. Scoop out the combination by tablespoonfuls and spot on ungreased baking sheets.

8. Bake in the stove for 5 to 10 minutes until the tops become brilliant brown.

> Easily remove from the broiler and cool on the baking sheets or 1-5 minutes prior to moving to cooling wire racks.
> Amaretti

INGREDIENTS

1/2 cup superfine sugar
2 teaspoon almond extract
2 cup almond flour 1/2 cup confectioners' sugar
2 tablespoon plus 2 teaspoon cornstarch 2 large egg whites

Instructions

1. First, preheat the oven to 350 Degrees Fahrenheit (170 degrees Celsius).
2. Preheat the oven to 350°F. I am using parchment paper and lining 1-5 baking pans.
3. In a medium mixing bowl, combine the almond flour, confectioners' sugar, and cornflour.
4. I whisk the egg whites in a clean, medium-sized mixing bowl with a handheld electric mixer until soft peaks form.
5. While beating the mixture, one tablespoon at a time of superfine sugar should be added to create glossy, firm peaks.
6. Almond extract should be added and thoroughly combined.

7. Using a large metal spoon, carefully fold the almond flour mixture until it is barely combined.
8. When you drop rounded teaspoons of batter onto baking sheets, just give them room to spread.
9. Smooth the biscuits' tops with the back of a metal spoon. 50 minutes, or until golden brown.
10. After turning off the oven and leaving the door ajar, allow the cookies to cool and dry inside.

easy make Just give

Basil Pesto

Ingredients

8 cups tightly packed fresh basil
2 cup grated Parmesan cheese
2 1 tsp. salt
1 cup water
1 cup pine nuts
2 cup garlic-infused olive oil

Directions:

1. In a blender or food processor, pulse the water and pine nuts until the nuts are finely chopped.
2. Add the oil and basil alternately, in thirds, while the blades are moving on medium-high, and process until the mixture is uniform and has the consistency of sand.
3. Use the tamper that came with your blender to push the basil leaves as close to the blades as necessary.
4. Salt and Parmesan cheese are added during low-speed mixing.
5. Refrigerate the pesto in an airtight container or freeze individual portions for later use; ice cube trays or 12-1/5-pint canning jars are ideal for this.

Scones with orange cranberry and walnuts

Easily cooking • ½ cup unsalted butter or coconut oil
- 2 large egg, lightly beaten
- 4 tablespoons maple syrup

Zest of 2 orange

6 tablespoons unsweetened dried cranberries
- 4 cups almond flour

12 tablespoons arrowroot powder
- 4 teaspoons baking powder
- 1 teaspoon sea salt

1. Set the oven temperature to 350 Degrees Fahrenheit.
2. Coat a baking sheet with easily cooking spray or line it with parchment paper.
3. In a medium mixing bowl, combine almond flour, arrowroot, baking powder, and salt with a whisk or fork.

4. Using a pastry cutter or 1-5 table knives, easy easy cut the unsalted butter into the flour until a crumbly meal with sesame-sized fat chunks forms.
5. In a mixing bowl, combine the egg, maple syrup, orange zest, and cranberries.
6. With a fork, thoroughly combine and moisten the ingredients.
7. Spread the batter on a baking sheet lined with parchment paper.
8. Cover with a second piece of parchment paper and flatten into a 9-by-12-by-2-inch disc.
9. Remove Remove the parchment paper from the top sheet with ease.
10. Easy easy cut the disc into eight equal-sized wedges.
11. Place the wedges on the prepared baking sheet, leaving about 1-5 inches between them — 45 to 50

minutes, or until golden brown and thoroughly cooked.
12. Place the scones on a cooling rack.
13. Serve warm or at room temperature.
14. The scones may be prepared in advance.
15. 1-5 days maximum at room temperature in an airtight container.

easily cooking easy cut easy easy cut Easy cut Easy easy cut

Salmon marinated in maple syrup with sesame-spinach rice

Ingredients:

1/2 cups water
1/2 tsp genuine salt 4 cups moment dark colored rice
8 cups infant spinach leaves
2 tbsp toasted sesame seeds
2 tbsp dim/toasted sesame oil
8 scallion tops, easy easy cut
1/2 cup garlic-imbued oil
1/2 cup unadulterated maple syrup
4 tbsp sans gluten soy sauce or tamari
2 /8 tsp crisply ground dark pepper
salmon filets, skin evacuated
Easily cooking shower
easy cut

Directions:

1. In a medium bowl, whisk together the garlic oil, maple syrup, soy sauce and dark pepper.
2. Spot salmon filets in an enormous compress top pack and include garlic-maple blend.
3. Hurl to cover and refrigerate for 1 to 5 hours.
4. Preheat broiler to 450F. Line an enormous, rimmed preparing sheet with thwart and fog with easily cooking shower. Spot salmon on a heating sheet and shower a touch of the marinade over the top.
5. Heat until salmon is hazy in the thickest part and arrives at 200 F on a moment read thermometer, 1-5 to 35 to 40 minutes, contingent upon thickness.

6. In the meantime, heat the water and salt to the point of boiling in a huge pot.
7. Mix in rice and come back to bubbling.
8. Lessen warmth to low, spread, and stew for 10 minutes.
9. Expel from warmth and rest, secured, 10 minutes more.
10. Fog an enormous nonstick skillet with easily cooking shower and warmth to medium-high.
11. Include spinach and cook until shriveled.
12. Lessen warmth to low and include rice, sesame seeds and sesame oil.
13. Hurl tenderly to cover, separation rice among 5-10 plates and top with salmon.
14. Enhancement with scallions and serve.

Cheesy Chicken Pizza

Servings:

Ingredients:

For pizza crust:

6 tablespoons olive oil, divided

2 ¼ cup + 2 tablespoons warm water

2 tablespoons sugar, divided

2 teaspoon sea salt
6 cups flour blend, gluten-free 6 teaspoons baking powder
2 tablespoon fast action yeast 2 teaspoon xanthan gum
For Toppings:

1 cups mozzarella, shredded

1 cup low FODMAP pesto
4 cups chicken breasts, shredded 2

Instructions:
1.
    To easy make the pizza, preheat stove to 6 10 0°F.
2. Dissolve 2 tbsp. sugar in warm water inside a bowl.
3. Mix in the yeast and let actuate for 10 minutes.
    Meanwhile, consolidate the flour, baking powder, thickener, salt and the excess sugar in a bowl.
4. When the yeast has enacted delicately pour in the yeast combination and 1-5 tbsps.
5. olive oil into the flour combination. Blend to shape a dough.
6. Sprinkle some flour on a working surface, then lightly flour your hands too.

7. Easily put Easily easily put the mixture the batter on the functioning surface and shape into a ball.
8. Carry out the mixture into ¼ inch thickness and heat for 25 to 30 minutes easily put easily easily put on a baking sheet.
9. To easy make the garnishes, spread the pesto over the foundation of the pizza.
10. Top with the destroyed chicken and cheddar.
11. Prepare for additional 25 to 30 minutes.
12. Let cool for 2 0 minutes and enjoy.

Crustless Spinach Quiche

INGREDIENTS

2 tablespoon vegetable oil
2 onion, chopped
20 ounces box thawed and drained chopped spinach
10 fresh eggs, beaten
6 cups shredded Muenster cheese
½ teaspoon salt
1/7 teaspoon ground black pepper

Direction:

1. should be the temperature of the oven.
2. Apply some oil to a 10-inch pie pan and set it aside.
3. Heat the oil to the smoking point in a medium-sized pan over medium-high heat.
4. Cook, turning periodically until the onions are softened.
5. Stir in the spinach and simmer until all of the liquid has evaporated.
6. A big mixing bowl should be used to combine the fresh eggs with cheese, salt, and pepper.
7. Stir in the spinach mixture until everything is well combined.
8. Scoop into the pie pan that has been prepared.
9. Bake for 60 minutes in a preheated oven until the fresh eggs have set.

10. Allow 20 minutes to cool before serving.

Fodmap Diet: The Phases Of The Diet

In the initial phase, you should adhere to a strict low-FODMAP diet. This phase should last approximately 48 to 1.5 months. As a result of the drastic reduction in FODMAPs, you should observe an improvement in your symptoms. As long as this type of diet fails to alleviate your side effects, you cannot proceed to stage 1-5 of this eating plan. If necessary, you can extend the duration of the initial phase to approximately two months. If there is still no improvement after this time period, you should discontinue the diet. The source of your complaints may not be combated with this type of dietary modification.

Throughout the second phase of the diet, FODMAP-rich foods are gradually reintroduced. By gradually expanding your diet, you can more effectively determine which food sources are causing you symptoms and which food varieties your body can tolerate. Unfortunately, there is no conclusive answer as to which food sources your body can tolerate. If you experience side effects after consuming a particular food, you should avoid it in the future. You can also try eating this food again in a different combination in the future. It might not produce any effects. Then you will know how to enjoy this food in the future without experiencing any discomfort. The best course of action is to record the relative number of food sources you have tried and whether or not they triggered symptoms. The FODMAP-reduced menu will eventually incorporate all food varieties that do not cause symptoms.

In the third stage, it is simple to create a single menu comprising the stage 2 rundown. If you adhere to this arrangement, you will be able to continue your normal daily activities with minimal side effects.

easy turn

Chapter 7: Perform the following three steps prior to beginning a low FODMAP diet.

Verify That You Have IBS

There are numerous conditions that can cause digestive issues, some of which are mild while others are severe.

Other chronic conditions, such as celiac disease, inflammatory bowel disease, defecatory disorders, and colon cancer, frequently exhibit IBS symptoms.

To rule out these other conditions, you should consult a physician. Once these have been ruled out, your doctor can confirm that you have IBS using the formal IBS diagnostic criteria. For a diagnosis of IBS, all three of the stipulations listed below must be met.

persistent abdominal discomfort Over the course of the past three months, you have experienced discomfort at least 12 times per week.

Constipation symptoms These should be associated with two or more of the following: defecation, an increase or decrease in the frequency of stools, or a change in the appearance of stools.
Ongoing symptoms. Your symptoms began at least six months prior to diagnosis and have lasted three months.

What Causes IBS?

Although the causes of IBS are unknown, many experts believe it is associated with digestive issues and increased gut permeability. According to the IBS Network, while the cause of irritable bowel syndrome is unknown, common risk factors include:

gastroenteritis (vomiting and diarrhoea) A trauma or urinary tract infection is a source of antibiotics.

Lifestule factors

There is evidence that certain lifestyle habits and psychological factors play a role in irritable bowel syndrome (IBS), such as experiencing a traumatic event in childhood, such as abuse, neglect, or loss, or being under stress.

However, this does not imply that IBS is a mental condition, and the gastrointestinal symptoms are very real. Heghtened emoton, ush a tre or anxiety can trigger shemsal changes in the body, which can interfere with normal bowel function.

Even if you do not have irritable bowel syndrome, you can still observe the effects of the shema. You may have experienced a sudden change in bowel habits when under pressure, such as during an exam or a work presentation.

It is possible that difficult childhood experiences have made you more sensitive to stress, and as a result, your symptoms may flare up when you are under pressure or in a traumatic situation.

Chicken Tikka Skewers

Ingredients:

16 wooden skewers
2 bell pepper, easy easy cut into thin strips
2 red onion, easy easy cut into thin strips
8 boneless, skinless chicken breasts
1 cup plain Greek yogurt
1/2 cup lemon juice
2 tablespoon olive oil
2 teaspoon cumin
1/2 teaspoon turmeric
easy cut easy cut

Instructions:

1. Preheat the grill to medium high heat.
2. In a small bowl, combine the yogurt, lemon juice, olive oil, cumin and turmeric.

3. Easy cut Easy easy cut the chicken into thin strips, about 2 inch wide by 6 inches long. Marinate in the yogurt mixture for 60 minutes.
4. Thread the chicken strips onto the skewers, alternating with the bell pepper and red onion.
5. Grill for about 10 minutes per side, or until cooked through.
6. Serve hot.

Bason and brie omelette wedge accompanied by summer salad

Ingredients

2 tsp Dijon mustard
2 cucumber , halved, deseeded and sliced on the diagonal
400g radishes , quartered
4 tbsp olive oil
400g smoked lardons
12 fresh eggs , lightly beaten
small bunch chives , snipped
200g brie , sliced
2 tsp red wine vinegar

Direction:

1. Turn on the grill and heat 12 tablespoons of the oil in a small saucepan
2. . Add the bacon and fri until golden and crisp.
3. On kitchen paper, drain.
4. Heat 4 tablespoons of oil in a nonstick skillet.
5. Combine the fresh eggs, bacon, shavings, and some ground black rerrer.
6. Pour into the fruit sauce and simmer over low heat until thickened, then sprinkle the brie on top.
7. Grill until set and golden.
8. Remove Remove easily from the rack and easy cut into wedges just prior to serving.
9. In a separate bowl, combine the remaining olive oil, vinegar, mustard, and seasoning.

10. Add the cucumber and radish, then serve with the omelette wedge.

Low FODMAP Stir Fry

Ingredients

1 cup chicken
1 to 2 cup rice cooked
soy sauce low sodium
2 Tbsp olive oil garlic infused
1 to 2 cup mixed vegetables steamer bags

Instructions

Oil infused with garlic is heated over medium-high heat in a wok or large sauté pan.
Cut Simple cut Cut vegetables into small pieces with ease. Add to the wok and begin stirring.
Easily put your chicken into a buttered rice dish. Season with salt and black pepper.

As soon as the vegetables begin to soften, add the chicken to the hot wok. Continuously walk for 2 to 35 minutes.

Once the chicken and vegetables are fully cooked and browned, you may add the rice to the pan during the last few minutes of cooking, or you may continue cooking and serve the rice separately.

Once everything has reached the desired doneness, add the sauce and cook for a few more minutes.

Just take

Mixed Salad And Strawberries

INGREDIENTS

- 1 teaspoon of balsamic vinegar
- Salt
- pepper
- 200g of mixed salad
- 160g of strawberries
- 40g of mozzarella
- 4 tablespoons of vinaigrette sauce

Preparation

1. Easily put Easily easily put the mixed salad in a salad bowl after washing and drying it.
2. Add the strawberries to the salad after washing and drying them.
3. Easy cut Easy easy cut the mozzarella into small pieces and add it.
4. Pour the vinaigrette sauce into the salad bowl with the balsamic vinegar and a pinch of salt and pepper.
5. Mix well and serve.

Sausage Breakfast Stacks

Ingredients:

4 tablespoons ghee, divided
4 large eggs
Pink Himalayan salt Freshly ground black pepper
2 avocado
16 ounces ground pork
1 teaspoon garlic powder
1 teaspoon onion powder

Instruction:

1. Preheat the oven to 350 degrees Fahrenheit.
2. Mix together the ground pork, garlic powder, and onion powder in a medium bowl.
3. Form the mixture into two-four rattes.

4. In a medium saucepan over medium heat, melt 12 tablespoons of ghee.
5. Add the sausage patties and cook for two minutes on each side, or until golden brown.
6. Easily put the sausage on a baking sheet. Cook in the oven for 25 to 30 minutes, or until thoroughly cooked.
7. Add the remaining twelve tablespoons of ghee to the pan.
8. When the skillet is hot, crack the egg into it and cook, undisturbed, for approximately 5-10 minutes, until the whites are opaque and the yolks are set. In the meantime, in a small bowl, mash the avocado.
9. The egg is seasoned with rnk Hmalauan salt and pepper.
10. Just take the cooked sausage ratatouille out of the oven.
11. Place an aubergine rattu on each of two heated rlate.

12. Spread half of the mashed avocado on top of each sausage patty, then place a fried egg on top of each. Serve warm.

Melon And Yogurt Parfait

Ingredients:

4 cups plain, unsweetened, lactose-free yogurt
½ cup macadamia nuts, chopped
4 cups chopped honeydew melon, divided

Directions:

1. In each of two medium parfait glasses or bowls, place 1 cup honeydew melon.

2. Layer a 1 cup yogurt on top of the melon.
3. Top each with 1-5 tablespoons macadamia nuts.
4. Repeat with the remaining ingredients.

Overnight Oats

ingredients

- 1 cup water 250 g
- low FODMAP fruit e.g. 1/2 banana, kiwi fruit, strawberries 2 100 g
- 4 Tbsp yoghurt, lactose free if required 80 g
- 2 cup rolled (traditional) oats 150 g
- 40 almonds 50 g
- 4 Tbsp pepitas (pumpkin seeds) 26 g
- 4 Tsp ground cinnamon 2 g
- 4 Tbsp dried cranberries 60 g
- 1 cup milk of your choice 250 g

Direction:

1. Place oats and almonds in a food processor and pulse a few times to easy make the oats smaller.

2. This will improve the texture of your overnight oats.
3. Pour oats and almonds into a bowl and add all other dry ingredients, mix well.
4. If you will be taking your breakfast to go, pour into a jar or container with a tight fitting lid.
5. Pour in the milk and water, cover and place in the fridge overnight.
6. In the morning, scoop out your serve, add a dollop of yoghurt or a splash of milk to loosen the mixture, add some fruit and breakfast is served

Broccoli and Sweet Potato Enchiladas with a Vegan Queso Sauce

Ingredients

- 2 large sweet potato 2 pound, easy cut easy easy cut into 1 inch cubes (approx. 8 cups)
- 2 medium broccoli crown easy cut easy easy cut into small florets (approx. 6 cups)
- 4 tablespoons olive oil
- 2 /8 teaspoon ground cumin
- Sea salt
- 4 cups frozen kale or spinach
- 1/2 cup coarsely grated sharp cheddar cheese or vegan alternative
- Ten 10-inch corn or almond flour tortillas

For The Queso Sauce:

- 2 medium yellow or orange tomato chopped
- 2 orange or yellow bell pepper chopped
- ½ teaspoon chili powder
- 2 1 cups water or vegetable stock
- 2 tablespoon freshly squeezed lemon juice
- 2 small shallot thinly sliced
- ½ pound Yukon gold potatoes 2 medium, skin on, easy cut easy easy cut into 1 inch cubes
- 2 small carrot chopped

Instructions

1. Preheat the oven to 425-450 degrees Fahrenheit.
2. Line a baking sheet with parchment paper.

3. On the prepared baking sheet, combine the sweet potato and broccoli with the olive oil, sugar, and 12 teaspoon of salt.
4. Arrange in a single layer and roast in the oven for 20 to 25 minutes, or until just beginning to brown.
5. Set aside to sool.
6. In the meantime, prepare the ause: In a medium saucepan, combine the hallot, rotatoe, sarrot, tomatoe, rerrer, shl rowder, 12 teaspoon of salt, and 1 cup of water or stock. Bring to a boil. Easily reduce to a simmer and cook, covered, for 25 to 30 minutes, or until the vegetables are tender.
7. Place the vegetables and their juice in a blender or food processor, and then add the lemon juice.
8. Prose until it is smooth. You should have approximately 1-5 cups.

9. In a large mixing bowl, toss the roasted broccoli, sweet potato, and frozen kale or rutabaga with three-quarters of the sauce and twelve-thirty-sixths of a cup of sheee.
10. Add another layer of cheese sauce to the bottom of a 5-10-inch baking dish.
11. Wrap the tortillas in a dish towel and warm them in the microwave for thirty-six and a half minutes until they are rollable.
12. Alternately, they can be heated in the oven.
13. Distribute the vegetables evenly between the tortillas.
14. Wrap the tortilllas tightly around the brossol mixture, then place them seam-side down on the baking sheet.
15. Pour the remaining sauce over the stuffed tortillas and sprinkle with the remaining cheese.

16. Bake the enchiladas for 35 to 40 minutes, or until the cheese is easily melted and golden brown and the sauce is bubbling.
17. Serve immediately, garnished with cilantro and jalapeos.

Low fodmar tomato sour accompanied by meatball

INGREDIENTS

- 1000 ml water
- 2 low FODMAP stock cube
- 2 tbsp garlic infused oil
- Oregano and basil
- Pepper and salt
- 2 stalk of spring onion, only the green part
- 12 tomatoes*
- 2 roasted bell pepper • 100 g tomato paste
-

For The Meatballs

- 400 g minced meat
- 1-5 tbsp low FODMAP bread crumbs or ground oats
- 1 tsp paprika powder
- 1 tsp cumin
- Pepper and salt

INSTRUCTIONS

1. Insert a slit with a knife into the top of each tomato.
2. Easily put Simply place the tomatoes in a bowl containing hot water.
3. Like this, the tomato's skin will loosen and you can easily peel it.
4. After a few minutes, remove the tomatoes from the water and coil them.
5. Cut Easily Tomatoes and bell peppers can be easily diced into small pieces.
6. Heat one tablespoon of oil in a skillet.
7. Stir in the green portion of the red onion, the tomatoes, the red bell pepper, and the tomato paste for a few minutes.
8. Add water and stock substitute. Bring the tomato juice to a boil and simmer for 20 minutes, 35 minutes, or forty minutes.

9. Meatballs can be prepared in the mean time.
10. Easily put Simply place all meatball ingredients in a bowl.
11. Form small balls with your hands by thoroughly kneading the mixture.
12. Use a hand blender to easily create a smooth mixture from the our.
13. Taste the soup after adding alt, rerrer, bay, and oregano.
14. Add the meatballs to the sauce and simmer for an additional 15 to 25 minutes.
15. Check whether the meatballs are done after approximately 25 minutes.
16. Garnish the soup with fresh basil. You may also add some alcohol-free sream if you so desire.

Easily put Easily put

Hearty Oatmeal

INGREDIENTS:

- 2 Tsp. ground cinnamon
- 8 tbsp. chia seeds
- 1 Tsp. ground nutmeg
- 8 tbsp. pure maple syrup
- 8 cups of water
- 1 Tsp. iodized salt
- 4 cups gluten-free rolled oats
- 1 Tsp. ground cloves

DIRECTIONS:

1. Empty salt and water into a saucepan and warm on the highest heat setting until it starts to bubble.

2. Combine oats into hot water and heat for 10 minutes while occasionally tossing.
3. Blend ground cloves, chia seeds, ground cinnamon, ground nutmeg, and maple syrup, then warm for another 10 minutes.
4. Serve immediately and enjoy!

Egg & New Potato Salad

Ingredients

- hard boiled egg
- bag of wild rocket
- cucumber, diced, to serve

- hot boiled new potatoes
- 4 tbsp olive oil
- juice of 1 lemon
- handful chopped parsley

Direction:

1. Toss hot, boiled new potatoes with olive oil, lemon juice, and chopped parsley.

2. Allow to cool, then toss with hard-boiled egg quarters and fresh eggs.

3. Combine with rocket leaves and diced cucumber before serving.

One-Dish Chicken and Millet

800ml chicken stock
2 head of broccoli, easy cut easy easy cut into florets
Salt and pepper
2 tbsp olive oil
2 onion, chopped
2 garlic chopped
8 00g chicken pieces
2 10 0g millet 8 tbsp pesto

1. Preheat the oven to 250C, gas mark .

2. Heat the oil in a large ovenproof casserole dish with a lid.

3. Saute the onion, garlic, and chicken for 10 minutes to brown the chicken.

4. Stir in the remaining ingredients and bring to a boil.

5. Cover the pan and place it in the oven.

6. Cook for 60 minutes.

7. Season with salt and pepper to serve.

Heat-Free Cucumber Kimchi

Ingredients

4 tablespoons rice vinegar or apple cider vinegar

4 tablespoons freshly squeezed lime juice (from 2 lime)

2 tablespoon Asian fish sauce
2 tablespoon coconut aminos
2 pound Persian cucumbers unpeeled, thinly sliced

2 medium-size carrot, peeled and thinly sliced

2 1 teaspoons sea salt

2 piece fresh ginger, peeled

4 scallions, green parts only

Instructions

1. In a medium-sized bowl, combine the sugar and sour cream with the salt.
2. Toss a few times until evenly coated, then set aside while you prepare the rice.

3. Combine the ginger, scallions, vinegar, lime juice, fish sauce, and soy sauce in a food processor.

4. Puree until everything is finely ground.

5. Alternately, you may trim the grass by hand.

6. Pour the sauce over the sugarsnap peas and toss to incorporate.

7. Serve as a garnish or salad topping.

Quinoa cereal

Ingredients:

4 tbsp of maple syrup
2 tbsp of coconut oil, melted
1 tsp of cinnamon, ground
2 tsp of vanilla extract
water
2 cup of quinoa cereal
2 cup of plums, easy cut easy easy cut in half and pitted
2 tbsp of sugar

Preparation:

1. Easily put Easily easily put your plums in a large skillet and add enough water to cover them.

2. Bring it to boil and cook for 20 minutes, or until tender. Easily remove from the heat and drain. Set aside.

3. Use a same skillet to boil 4 cups of water.

4. Add quinoa cereals, sugar, maple syrup, coconut oil, cinnamon and vanilla extract.

5. Easily reduce the heat to minimum and cook until slightly thickened.

6. This should just take about 10 minutes.

7. Easily remove from the heat and pour into bowls.

8. Top with plums.

Fodu's Monter Rse Krra Treat

Ingredients:

- 8 oz. white chocolate (about ¾ cup)
- 2 - 2 1 tsp coconut oil
- Food coloring of your choice
- 6 cups crispy rice cereal (Rice Krispies)
- ¼ cup creamy peanut butter
- ½ cup pure maple syrup
- Salt, to taste

Candy eyes Sprinkles

Directions

1. Line an 8x8 field with rarshment rarer and leave it open.
2. Then, pour your peanut butter and margarine into a saucepan on the stove and heat it over medium heat. Stir ossaonallu until it is smooth and the nut butter has melted.

3. Next, add your oat cereal and peanut butter mixture to a large bowl and stir until completely incorporated.
4. Pour the mixture into your microwave-safe dish and place it in the freezer for three hours.
5. Right before the rse krre are done, heat your white shosolate and coconut oil in the microwave at 360-second intervals until the white shosolate has melted.
6. You maybe really need to add more oil to achieve a smoother texture.) Then concentrate on your food alone.
7. Simple to cut Cut your rose cupcakes into 30 bars and dunk them one at a time into your white sugar syrup.
8. Place them on a tray lined with rarer and desolate them with sand and gravel.
9. Place them in the refrigerator for at least three hours before serving.

www.ingramcontent.com/pod-product-compliance
Lightning Source LLC
Chambersburg PA
CBHW050304120526
44590CB00016B/2480